Growing
Lifetime Value

RETENTION & RENEWAL

Sandra S. Fox

Investment Copy Publisher
Mountain Home, Arkansas

Investment Copy Publishing
2288 Old Tracy Rd
Mountain Home, AR 72653
www.InvestmentCopy.com

Book Layout ©2015 BookDesignTemplates.com

Ordering Information:
Quantity sales. Special discounts are available on quantity purchases by corporations, associations, and others. For details, contact the "Special Sales Department" at the address above.

Growing Customer Lifetime Value: Retention & Renewal/ Sandy Fox —1st ed.
ISBN 978-0-9907138-2-1

Table of Contents

Dedicated to all the hard working marketers and copywriters who want to bring service and benefits to their customers.

If you want your business to move to the top and create real success and wealth, you have to do more than just write to attract or even sell.
You have to create high levels of rapport, trust, and relationships. You have to sustain your customers' interests on a continuing basis.

—**Dan S. Kennedy** *No BS Marketing, GKIC*

CHAPTER 1

Why You Lose Customers

Most businesses focus their time and energy on customer acquisition. You need to get customers in the front door—whether it's brick and mortar or on a website—or you'll soon go out of business.

Usually those customers cost money to acquire. Incentives. Bonuses. Free trials. The cost of the advertising that got them to come to you in the first place. In the past, once you got clients in the door and you offered them great value... they were likely to stay.

But with competition and easy marketing via email and the internet, more and more customers are less loyal. They seek the best new deal. They ask themselves: what's in it for me? So when they come across a promise of even better outcomes... they jump ship and sign up.

How can you change fickle customers into a loyal fan club? What can you do to insure your best clients keep doing business with you? It's more than offering a valuable product. It's about focusing on retention and renewals of subscriptions or continuity programs.

Ask yourself: What is the value of the customer coming in the front door... if they soon leave out the back door and never return?

How much money are you leaving on the table through lack of follow-through? Some marketers put this number at 200% or more.

Nurture Your Customers

Nurturing your customers and helping them to decide to stay with you benefits your company. A system of focused follow-up can double or triple the customer lifetime value.

Look at your customers. How much lifetime value do they bring to you right now?

- If you could get them to renew for 2-3 more years... what would that mean to your business?
- If they loved you and trusted you enough to buy additional products... how much more value would they bring you?
- If customers were so devoted, they recommended you to their friends...how would that affect your bottom line?

What would that extra money mean to your company, your lifestyle, your growth?

As you read this book, you will find a system of specific steps you can take to retain your customers. Many are low cost and easy to implement. Some you may be doing within existing programs. And just by tweaking it a little you can build that loyalty which will generate more revenue. Other steps may involve a change of attitude... or even a change in the way you acquire your customers.

You need not incorporate all the best practices for retention in order to see a significant change in your customer lifetime value.

Indeed, I encourage you to pick and choose among the ideas for those that fit your situation the best. Open your vision to ideas from other business models. For example, loyalty cards work well for some retail stores. Can you find a way to adapt them to your online business?

Create your personalized system for retaining customers.

Place a strong focus on retaining your customers. When you design retention and renewals to help them want to subscribe and stay in your continuity programs, you build a fence around your business that protects you from competitors. It helps recession-proof your business. And it keeps more money in your pocket.

CHAPTER 2

Infusing Retention into Your Business Model

Businesses benefit when they take retention into consideration in every decision they make. As soon as you get a customer, your thought should be: how can I keep this customer. You lose a tremendous amount of money when you have a "one-and-done" business model.

Even with occasional sales like auto and home, savvy sellers keep the door open. In this information age, it's easy to invite your customers to stay close.

Branding. You have a unique selling position that attracted your customer in the first place. What can you do to increase their understanding of your unique value? What other steps can you take to make your business more visible and more attractive to your customers?

Contact. Stay in touch with your customer. Help them remember you. Encourage them to recognize how happy they've been with their wise decision to buy from you. Here are several ways to stay in touch on a regular basis.

- Email follow up series
- Newsletters

- Coupons or special offers
- Valuable content

Value. In this increasingly competitive world, make sure your value is of the highest quality. When you know your clients-- what they need and want-- you can better tailor your content to be perceived as extremely valuable to them. Make sure your content and your offers are worth their attention—every time.

Appreciation. It's tempting to look on your transactions as... well, a business deal. But in this impersonal world, the personal touch gets noticed. It's valued and sets you apart. Courtesies move the sale from business deal into a relationship. Always take time to thank your customers and say it in a way that feels honest and honoring.

Make those individual buyers friends, and they'll stick with you. Increase the relationship with acts such as:

- Genuine thanks and appreciation
- Recognition of important events—birthdays, membership anniversaries, holidays
- Reaching out with personal emails or phone calls.
- Surveys or opinion polls to find out their thoughts and values

Front Sales. Often newsletters—especially financial newsletters—are sold on the bonuses. Continuity programs may be sold on a special introductory training. There is a risk to emphasizing the upfront bonus in the promo without spending as much time selling the newsletter or continuity program.

If you sell the bonus too strongly, buyers will do anything to get the bonuses... including signing up for the newsletter or continuity program. Of course you say they can keep the bonus, even if they cancel. So buyers use the bonuses, but pay no attention to the newsletter you want them to subscribe to. Naturally, when it comes time to renew, they cancel.

You can reduce this attrition in the sales letter. Make sure to sell the newsletter and its expert as much as you sell the bonuses. Focus on performance, value, and benefits others have achieved with it. Highlight the expert and his or her track record, passion, knowledge, skill, and dedication to the success of the customer.

As soon as the sale is made, the work of retention begins.

CHAPTER 3

Engage Your Subscribers

One time a well-known speaker sent blank CD's to his customers by mistake. It was supposed to be a recording of his latest training. When he discovered the mistake, he was horrified. He waited for the cry of alarm he expected from the buyers. To his astonishment, he got surprisingly few returns. How could this be?

He realized few people actually took the time to listen to the CD's. Even though they ordered them and paid for them… they never used them.

If your customers never open the newsletter, never engage in the continuity program, never buy a stock pick or execute an action you recommend, they are not engaged. They won't see the value. They will not renew.

Start the Day They Order

As soon as you send your product, you need to encourage your customers to take action. Here are eight ways you can keep your customers engaged from the get-go.

1. Welcome Them. Let them know you appreciate their trust in you and you promise to serve them well. Reaffirm your track record and promote your expert. Announce your successes and be sure to remind them of your guarantee.

Help them see your dedication to their success as you call attention to all of the benefits they will get.

Don't settle for a generic welcome. Seek to make it personal sounding and as genuine as you can. You want to start building a relationship.

2. Remind and Set Expectations. Review with your new customer the benefits they can expect to receive with your product. Tell them what it will look like and how to use it to get the maximum results. Explain what they can expect from it and when they can anticipate seeing the results they want.

3. Invite Feedback. When they are in the bliss of buying, invite them to write down their goals. Encourage them to share on a forum or on your website about their purchase and what they see it doing for them. Keep them forward looking to the benefits that come from using the program.

4. Surveys or Questionnaires. You begin building a relationship with your customers when you listen to what they say. Asking for input helps them feel like you care about them and their opinions.

You can ask:

- What did they like about the product?
- What do they hope or expect it to do for them?
- What can we do to make this even better for you?
- How can we help you get the most value from this?
- What do you expect to use this for?
- What similar programs like this have you used in the past? What worked well? What didn't?

- What questions do you have that we haven't answered?

Surveys are a two way street. You help readers engage and start to focus on your product. You also gather information that will help you improve your product and add even more value to you customers.

Surveys alert you to possible shortcomings in your product. They can show you where your customers want more— so you can develop new products.

5. Share the Process. Engage subscribers by giving them an insider's view into the expert's process. For example, create a short video of the expert going into greater depth on how he gets the successes he does. This will create a greater desire in the buyer to act on what they purchased. They will gain confidence that the process will work for them.

6. Testimonials or Case Studies. Social proof is powerful. When readers see others finding success, they gain confidence they can too. It increases their desire and their likelihood of taking action. It may show them the steps they need to take to create that success.

7. Offer Helpful Content. This step is easy. It's what attracted your prospect to you. Ideally your newsletter or continuity program excels at giving your customers vital content.

8. Be Consistent. Continue the same conversation you began in the sales letter. All communications immediately following the buy will benefit if they carry through the same big idea, the same tone of voice, and the same promises as in the sales letter. Recognize the emotions and the painful problem addressed in the promo. Those are the things that got your buyers to click "Order."

You resonated with their feelings, fears, and needs. If you change the tone of the communication, you run the risk that your buyer will think they have made a mistake. Maybe you don't really understand them as well as they thought you did.

Set up a System to Keep Customers Close

The first way to connect with and engage your buyers is after the order page. You'll send them a welcome letter or a way to access the product they purchased.

Next, send a series of emails. These use a blend of the ideas suggested above. The order of emails might look something like this:

Day 1. Give them a welcome letter reminding them of ways to access their information. You'll also remind them of the good decision they made and how pleased they will be with it. At the same time, you might send them to an orientation before they get their first issue.

Day 3. Send a short video of the guru welcoming them to the program. He might share some of his process and express delight that they will be working together.

Day 6. Send a testimonial or case study.

Day 10. Are there any complexities to using your program, taking action in your newsletter, or executing a trade? Give them bonus training on how to do it. Make it easy for them to take action.

Day 16. Encourage them to engage. Send a survey or questionnaire. Ask them if they've gotten started. Ask if they have any questions. Is there anything you can do to help them?

Day 30. Send a testimonial or case study. Invite them to share their successes with the guru and give them a way to do so.

You don't want to overwhelm your subscriber with too many emails. At the same time, your contact should send the message: *I care about your success. I want to help you. This program will do great things for you. Get started and see the results for yourself.*

When your subscribers feel valued and cared for, they will want to stay with you.

CHAPTER 4

Cultivate a Relationship

You may think that the continuity you offer automatically creates a relationship. You have an expert, a guru sending out important information on a regular basis. It has the power to change the lives of your readers.

Yet the more you strengthen this relationship, the more you eliminate any competition to your product. Take a look at your newsletter or the continuity program and see if you can come across stronger in these areas.

Act with Honesty. Always be upfront and honest with your customers. Sometimes mistakes happen. Be real about it. Mistakes make you seem more human and more real and likeable.

Customers are much more likely to forgive a mistake than they will a cover-up. Use it as a teaching tool and a learning experience for everyone.

Keep Your Promises. Make sure your program keeps all the promises made in the sales letter. Customers will trust you, believe you and follow you longer when your promises are truthful and not hype.

Be Genuine Real people don't try to be better or more important or smarter than they really are. Being themselves is good enough—warts and all.

Genuine people are also real with their emotions. They value their customers and think of them as people who need their services... not as marks, dollar signs or a commodity.

Respect Your Readers. Respect their time, their intellect, their needs, wants, and desires. Be patient with their quirks and biases. Give them the benefit of the doubt.

If you feel condescending toward your subscribers, it will come out in your material. People can spot a fake.

Be Likeable. The attributes above will make you likeable. When you genuinely care about your readers, they will reciprocate and genuinely care about you and be loyal to you.

In this age of social media and reality television, people like to know about the personal lives of those they interact with. Your expert becomes more real and more likeable as he or she shares small bits of personal life—vacations, hobbies, family, even favorite foods.

It can be a simple "throw-away line" such as, I'm not recommending this stock because of my deep love of chocolate, but technical analysis shows Nestle is a good value now.

Act Unique and Quirky. Part of your unique selling position is who you are or who your expert is. If that expert looks like all the other experts around—says the same thing, does the same thing—it's easy to lose out to the competition.

It's your differences that make you unique. Flaunt them. Make them a part of your newsletter, your continuity program, your business. Wear hiking boots. Grow a handlebar moustache. Use purple ink.

Even in conservative financial publications you can stand out and be... well... quirky. Teeka Tiwari of Jump Point Trader lets his personality shine through. He calls himself "Big T" and has a sign off slogan: *Let the game come to you.*

If you think of your newsletter or continuity program strictly as a business venture on a professional level, you are missing the human element. It's possible and essential to compete using outstanding products and services. Yet, you'll find building a more personable relationship will cement client loyalty through any problems or glitches.

Demonstrate Customer Building Qualities

How can you most easily demonstrate some of these qualities? Emails are simple and can be effective if carefully crafted.

Videos increase effectiveness as they add voice, face, and increased personality. Videos are an ideal way to showcase the above qualities. Followers can hear the sincerity and genuineness in your voice. They see you and come to like you more. You can share your quirkiness in your personality.

Webinars, conference calls, and even pre-recorded calls also can build the relationship. When we communicate, our words convey only 7% of the communication. The rest is in inflection, tone of voice, body language and other non-verbal forms of communication.

Doesn't it make sense to take advantage of video or audio to better communicate with your customers?

What might you do in a video webinar, conference or pre-recorded call?

- Teach how to do something—analyze a stock, solve a problem or master an aspect of their goal
- Explain a principle in greater depth
- Review the portfolio
- Introduce a new service or stock pick

- Remind readers of an upcoming event

Most of the strategies we've been talking about up to now are mono-directional. They go from you to the subscriber. The more you can create an avenue for two-way dialogue, the more you will capture the hearts and minds (and wallets) of your clients.

Encourage Feedback

How can you encourage feedback? Sure, you ask for it in your newsletters, but what else can you do? First you can respond to that feedback in the newsletter. When you print the comments in the next newsletter along with your response to the comment, you create a sense of community. All your readers feel validated and important... not just the one who wrote in.

Here are more ways to encourage feedback.

- When you create the videos, ask for comments. Make sure there's a comment section on the page and ask listeners to give feedback in the comment section.
- Offer question and answer time at the end of the webinar or conference call. Or even make the entire event a Q&A time.
- When you invite comments in emails and newsletters, use the PS to say, *'Yes. I mean it. I really want to hear back from you. I want to serve you better and your feedback helps me do that."*
- Businesses are starting to use "stay" interviews. They call top employees and ask them why they stay. What is the company doing right? What might entice them to leave? Then they use that information to build a culture to keep that employee. Do the same for your subscribers.

- Make it easy to give feedback. Don't make your subscribers click several times, navigate different pages or sign in to leave a comment. Insure your system is user-friendly.

- Use quizzes, surveys, games, and rewards to get feedback from key subscribers. Then acknowledge these responses. Let readers know the results of the survey. Answer specific questions in the newsletter or on a page on the website. Let readers feel their opinions are valuable and appreciated. For an example, look at Brad Hoppmann's *Uncommon Wisdom Daily* (Afternoon Edition). He is particularly good about responding to subscriber comments and incorporating feedback into his next day's issue.

- Ask questions when they exit. I know that many newsletters say, "We'll refund your subscription, no questions asked." But you're missing a valuable opportunity. Promise the refund. Let them know you are processing it. Then say, "We try to provide excellent value to our subscribers. Is there anything we could have done to have made the service more valuable to you?"

Remember that all this relationship building and communication is a great way to collect testimonials. As you invite responses be SURE to save all the positive feedback you get. If necessary, follow up one-on-one with readers who give great feedback.

Testimonies are gold when it comes time to renew subscriptions! Even if you need to assign someone to call the subscriber and ask deeper questions... it's worth it!

Relationships develop as people and businesses get to know each other better. Review your business and look for ways you can deepen relationships with your customers. It will pay dividends in retention and renewals.

CHAPTER 5

Rescuing At-Risk Customers

How many times do your subscribers join... and then do nothing with the product? When that happens they are simply a cancelation waiting to happen.

When you have programs that can identify this group and segment them out, you have a way to step in and rescue these customers. Once you have identified them, what can you do?

Here are five ways to re-engage and recover customers who have taken no action.

1. Find Out Why

There are many reasons people buy and don't use. They get busy. They lose the password. Life changes. They tried it and had a bad experience. It no longer fits their lifestyle.

While many of these reasons are possible, the most likely is that they got busy. Chances are that the problem that led them to purchase your product is still there. They still have that worry, concern or pain point. They still want to fix that problem. This means: THEY STILL NEED YOUR PRODUCT!

Perhaps they tried it briefly and felt like it didn't work for them. Most likely, they haven't tried it at all. Procrastination. Fear. Time. Indecision. Confusion. There are many reasons we don't do things we want to or think we should be doing.

If it's possible to discover the reason for the inaction, your chances of re-engaging them are better. The most direct way is to ask them. Sometimes you'll even get a truthful answer.

The trick is to make it easy for them to respond... and fun... and worth it. Surveys, games, quizzes and offering prizes all help engage. They will lead to answers. How you phrase the questions — and their quantity— is also key to getting a response.

- Tell them exactly how many questions and how long the quiz or survey will take.

- Promise them a benefit. A benefit might be that you'll hear their opinions; they matter to you. Or maybe you'll send a free report, discount offering or gift. Everyone evaluates their actions by the "what's-in-it-for-me" rule. Make it worth their time.

- Create questions they'll want to answer:
  - ➢ If you had 15 minutes to spend with [your guru] what questions would you want to ask him/her?
  - ➢ What can we do to help you take full advantage of [program]?
  - ➢ What's holding you back from taking full advantage of [benefits] we have for you?
  - ➢ What do you see as your next step to [achieve the promise of the program—double digit gains, grow your wealth, save money…etc.]

> ➤ When you signed up for [program] likely you hoped to accomplish [solution]. How is that going for you? What are you doing now to accomplish that? What can we do to help?
>
> ➤ What is your biggest worry about [what the program offers] now? How can we help you move ahead?

At the end of the survey, invite re-engagement. Tell them what a next step is. People want to be guided by mentors they trust. Offer a hint or tip for fast starting. Give some resources to help them move forward. The resources or training might be part of the bonus or promise you make to get them to take the survey. But always end with guidance on the next move for your reader.

Both the survey and the following items are most effective when they are part of an email series. Often readers need several reminders before they take action. And, indeed, learning why they are not taking action is only part of the problem.

Consider sending the survey, then some follow up reminders to truly reengage your at-risk customers. The reminders in your email series could have some of the following elements in them. You can mix and match.

2. Teach Them a Skill

Why haven't they taken action? Maybe they are unsure of the next steps. Maybe they don't understand the "why" behind the actions. You can easily go into depth in one area to get them started again.

Engage them in the program. Perhaps they need a tutorial to help them understand the features of your continuity program. A short screen-share video can re-introduce them to the steps to moving forward.

Introduce tools to make it easier. Perhaps you have a simple system for choosing the right option pricing. Demonstrate it in a step-by-step process to your customers. You will increase their confidence and their desire to put it to work making them money.

Maybe you have a spread sheet or an analyzing calculator or some other simple chart, evaluator or tool that will make using your newsletter or program easier for your client. Share that with them.

Explain the inner workings. Take a small part of you program, your philosophy, methodology and peel back the curtain. Let readers understand why or how the newsletter comes up with the recommendations it does. Ideally it would be easy to understand. But even complex algorithms that clients don't understand, can give them reassurance that YOU understand them and are using the technical analysis for their benefit.

Or you might review the "why" behind why it's important they take action. When you explain again the "what's in it for me?" factor, you increase their desire to act.

---

3. Tell Them Stories

Everyone loves a story. As human beings we are hard-wired to listen to the end of the story. They draw us in and build relationships. They create trust. And they encourage us to act.

Testimonials are the easiest stories. Each testimonial carries that personal involvement that creates resonance. When readers see other people like them succeeding, they are encouraged to try it, too.

Not all testimonials are created equal. The following is a less effective testimonial:

"You guys did a great job. I'll keep using you." – B. J., Texas

It is vague and non-specific. You know little about the person or the company. A better testimonial is like a mini-case study. If possible, create a fuller story. Have them say:

➢ What was life like before the product?

➢ What have they done with the product?

➢ What are the results? How is their situation better or different now?

➢ How do they feel about it?

It might look something like this:

"I was flooded with conflicting financial advice. And so much of it turned out to be bad. Then I heard about the Best Financial Newsletter and their safe stocks. I started following your advice. I've had such peace of mind as I've watched my portfolio increase a solid 10% in just the last year.'- Jim Franks, Kansas City, MO

Tell your story or the story of your guru. Many online marketers have a rags-to-riches story. Those, of course, are very engaging. But you can tell other stories that will let readers get a glimpse into your life, your personality, your family, your methods, and your ideals. You might share:

• One of your success stories

• The success of one of your students or clients

• One of your failures and how it led to a break-through and a better product

• A thought or principle you learned—and how it affects your business

4. Remind Them of Value

Send a series of emails that reminds them of the great value of what they signed up for. Re-sell them on the product or newsletter. Rekindle their worry, concern and pain points plus the interest and the excitement they felt when they first discovered your product.

Insure that your continuity program is full of great content that in a very real way will resolve the problem or concern they are currently facing. Make it easy for them to uncover and use the content you offer. Show them statistics, testimonials, charts and graphs that reinforce the value they are receiving.

5. Give Them a Gift

It's almost expected to get extra bonuses when you subscribe. However, a gift out of the blue—undeserved and unexpected—is very attractive. It engages the law of reciprocity. It creates a sense of curiosity. If they've received this great gift... what have they missed by not participating in the newsletter or continuity program?

The gift can be physical or informational. It may be that you can frame some of the other activation options as gifts. Your free training or your short video of your guru's story can be structured as a gift. Remember, for a gift to be fully appreciated, it must have NO STRINGS ATTACHED.

Customers are jaded. They've seen nearly all "free gifts" come with strings. They, at minimum, need to give their name and email for the gift. They may need to listen to a sales presentation or sign up for a continuity program.

Send a gift just for friendship's sake— just because they are subscribers to the newsletter. Personalize your email if at all possible. Sample text might look like this:

Hey, [name]. Because you're part of our [newsletter or continuity program] family, I know you're interested in [subject.] I came across this [gift/report/bonus] and I just wanted to send it out as our thank you for being a [subscriber/member]. Enjoy!

Make sure you also personalize the "from" line. It needs to look like it comes from a real person. Make it from John.Smith@BestPub.com not Editor@BestPub.com or BestPub@BestPub.com.

Mix and match these methods to re-engage your at-risk customers. You will remind them about you and why they liked you enough to buy in the first place. You will build and deepen the relationship and you will be much more likely to retain the customer.

CHAPTER 6

Preparing for the Renewal

B ill sees an email pop up. His *Best Financial Newsletter* subscription is about to automatically renew and they're going to charge his credit card $99 in two weeks.

Bill's finger hovers over the delete button. He thinks, *how much have I read and used that newsletter? Do I really need it? $99. Hmmm.*

Your goal is to have Bill... and all your clients delete the auto-renew notice thinking, *Yeah, I NEED that. $99? That's such a good deal. It's a no brainer.*

If you don't have auto-renew for your continuity program, you need to plan the renewal process even more carefully. Now, rather than having inaction become your friend, it's your enemy. You need your customers to take action for their subscription to renew.

Whether you have an automatic or manual renewal program in place in your business, the month before the renewal month is a time to refocus on your clients.

If you have been doing some of the things mentioned in previous chapters to build the relationship—surveys, testimonials, trainings and so on—then you can just continue those communications into the renewal. You have already built the relationship.

If not, in the tenth month you need to reconnect and strengthen the relationship so when the renewal comes, your customers automatically click "yes!" Prepare your subscribers to say YES at renewal time with these events.

- **Surveys**- Get a pulse on how your customer has interacted with your continuity program or newsletter. What have they liked about it? What more would they like from you?
- **Testimonials**– Send out testimonials as social proof for how others have successfully used the information.
- **Surprise gift**-- When a gift is sent 4- 6 weeks in advance of the renewal letter it is disconnected enough so it does not seem like a bribe. It looks like a gift freely given. Yet the reciprocity urge still lingers in the customers mind. They still have those warm feelings toward you when the renewal comes around.

Plan the Upsell. Dan Kennedy, founder of *No BS Marketing*, says that 20% of your customers want to buy more from you. They want the premium package. They love you, they love your stuff, and they want more of it.

What are you doing to offer them more? There are a variety of options:

- Longer subscriptions. Move from monthly to annually, or 1 year to 5 years
- More frequent information. Try daily advice instead of weekly or monthly
- More detailed information. Offer more specific portfolio help, more step-by-step instruction, more in-depth reports, books
- "Done For You" programs. Is there more you can do for your customers to lighten their burden. Perhaps you part-

ner with a brokerage house that invests their money according to your portfolio and your stops

- Access to online training
- Upgrading to webinars and group coaching
- One-on-one training or coaching

Consider the Down-sell. You will have some customers that will not renew. Can they be salvaged? Can you offer them some product at a lower price point that might keep them as a customer?

- Shorter subscription— perhaps 3 months or 6 months
- Bare bones or parts of an unbundled service
- Single event items- books, webinars, back office library
- More limited material—a newsletter that goes out monthly instead of weekly or daily
- Special highlights series—breaking trends, making sense of the news that is more periodic

When you prepare in advance, you are ready to respond when you learn your customer's renewal preferences. Again, questionnaires can help you segment your customers to better target their needs.

CHAPTER 7

Writing the Renewal Letter

What is the purpose of the renewal letter? It seems obvious. But there's more to it than just getting the money. And if you focus strictly on completing a business transaction, you may lose sales.

An effective renewal letter will do several things in addition to clearly stating renewal options. It will:

Express Appreciation. You've had this customer for a period of time. Thank them. Appreciate their trust and confidence in you. Be grateful for the relationship.

Remind Them. Remind them of their problem and how your newsletter or continuity program is helping them resolve that problem. Remind them what they are getting for their money.

Offer Proof. Give some facts or statistics to back up your/their success. Use testimonials to show benefits.

Show Respect. Respect their intellect, their needs and wants, and their hard-earned money.

Use Emotion. Go back to the sales letter that got them into your program. What were the ideas and the emotions that resonated with them at that time? Use it again.

Give Directions. Tell your readers exactly what you want them to do. Click to quickly renew? Ignore and let the process proceed? Fill in the blanks? Make it clear and easy to follow.

Because you are dealing with current customers you can be more direct. They know you. Hopefully they've developed a relationship with you and used your product. When they are rabid fans, all you have to do is show them the terms and say, "click here to renew." These ultra-faithful need little encouragement.

But what about your fence-sitters? How can you craft a renewal letter that will turn them into eager buyers? Here are seven ways to sway them to renew.

---

1. The "From" Line

With email, you have the benefit of the "from" line. If you have a good relationship with your client, they will open the email because they know, like, and trust you.

Help your customers feel the relationship and the tone of the letter with your choice in the "from" line. Is it from *Best Financial Newsletter?* Avoid having it come from the parent company as readers have less of a relationship with that company.

Better still, draw on a relationship tone and have the specific name of your editor or guru in the "from" line. Of course the tone of the email will continue in the voice of your newsletter editor.

If your clients typically get several emails from you every day, your subject line needs to alert them that this one is different and critical.

If you are sending direct mail, look carefully at the return address. Do you want it from the business? From the guru? Do you want to leave it blank... so readers must open the letter to learn who is sending it?

2. Headline or Subject Line

You have just a few words for readers to decide if what you are offering has sufficient value to them. With a headline in a direct mail renewal you can make it longer and offer more benefits. You can add an outside envelope teaser to increase their chances of opening the letter.

With emails, most effective subject lines are short and catchy. Successful subject lines do one or more of these things.

- ✓ Offer a benefit
- ✓ Create curiosity
- ✓ Give information
- ✓ Use numbers
- ✓ Look odd or quirky
- ✓ Are personalized

You may want to begin with a straight forward subject line. I'm a fan of personalized subject lines. When you see your own name it just calls to you. You are attracted to it and you at least read the subject line.

The only danger here is that some people do not give the name they typically use. If everyone calls them Bob and your email is addressed to Robert, it ends up being less personal. Or if they put down a different name to avoid spammers and the subject line reads, Hey, Stupid... it won't create the tone you hope for.

If you send a series of emails for your renewal, change up the subject line. First, give them a straight forward subject line: Hi Jim! *Best Financial Newsletter* is ready to renew.

If that doesn't get opened and acted upon, your follow up subject lines can draw from successful ideas others have used.

Benefits:

- ✓ Jim, Ready to claim your free [bonus]?

✓ Jim, want another seven bagger?

✓ Jim, here's your insurance against wild market swings

Curiosity:

✓ Check out this CRAZY discount

✓ Jim—Are you one step away from success?

✓ The wealth grower's secret weapon…

Information:

✓ Jim… 9 ways to make 210% returns this year

✓ Jim, your personal method to build a winning portfolio…

✓ Three steps guaranteed to reduce your market risks

Follow-up

✓ Jim, did you miss this?

✓ Just checking back—this is important

✓ Re: your renewal bonus

---

3. Lead or Introduction

The first sentence or two in your email are critical. In many email servers, you can see the first part of the sentence in the preview line. Readers may decide to click or not click based on that fragment.

Next, your introduction must continue the promise and tone begun in the subject line. Readers reject bait-and-switch with a passion. So while your subject line needs to create curiosity and draw them in, the first lines of the email must reinforce or refer back to the message of the subject line.

Perhaps you've heard of the ruse where the. Subject line said *"FREE SEX."* In the text it continued: *Now that I have your attention let me tell you about our amazing computer sale!* Your readers feel rightly angered and betrayed with this bait and switch.

If the subject line offers an elite opportunity, the body must continue that elite theme. If the subject line is quirky and offbeat, make sure the body does not take a formal tone. Your lead or introduction lets readers know they've arrived at the right place. They feel the continuity.

4. The Body of the Letter

As you prepare to write the renewal, refer back to the original sales offer. Look at what motivated the customer to buy in the first place. What was the big idea? What promise did the letter make? What inner feelings did it tap into?

Those were powerful enough to get your customer to buy the first time. Incorporate some of those ideas, promises, benefits, and emotions into this shorter renewal letter.

It is to your advantage to know your customers more than demographically and superficially. The more you understand their core emotions, wants, and desires, the better you can be at helping them see how this renewal will satisfy those needs. It's not all about fear or greed. There are many reasons people want to improve their lives.

Why do your readers want to accumulate wealth or accomplish what your continuity program promises? It could be so they can better care for their family. It might be so they can stay ahead of the competition. Or look good and be admired. Perhaps they are afraid of running out of money in retirement and living in poverty. Maybe they want to leave a legacy for their children.

These are vital, powerful emotions. When you strike a chord with their deepest emotions, it resonates. They feel it. They WANT the solution you offer. They become eager buyers. They are anxious to renew.

If your message is written in the voice of your editor, check for the number of "I's" in the text. It's a great indicator of whether the message is company directed or customer directed. Clients are most concerned about themselves—their money, their quality of life, their problems and successes.

They care about the company only to the degree that it helps them. The uppermost question is: What's in it for me? All of the email should be written from that perspective. Rather than:

> *I'll show you how to pick the stock poised for rapid growth...*

Say:

> *You'll quickly see how to pick the stock poised for...*

The more you can change "I" sentences to "you" sentences the more you will capture and engage your readers. They will see the benefits more clearly. It will more directly answer their unspoken question: How does this benefit me?

You hope your readers have benefited from the actions you recommended in your newsletter. Then it's easier to sell the renewal. But some people buy the dream. They buy the promise and the desire to achieve. Maybe they haven't really used it yet... but they want to and plan to.

Therefore, it's important to revisit what the program has done for others and can do for them. This proof reminds them why it's such a good deal for them. You can focus on:

- **The credentials of your guru or expert**. What qualifies him to lead your readers?
- **Past performance**. How have the recommendations of the expert performed over the last year? Or since he or she began the service?

- **Outside experts.** Quotes about your expert or the service from The Wall Street Journal or other prestigious sources add credibility.
- **Testimonials.** A great advantage of testimonials is that they are people like your reader sharing their success and what it means to them. Here you can draw upon the core emotions that your reader can connect with—saving enough to retire comfortably, no-stress investing, confidence in the face of market swings. The confidence of the testimonial writer transfers to your client. And they feel more comfortable renewing.

When you work to create a powerful body to your copy with all these elements included, your reader wants to buy from you.

5. Your Guarantee

Give your strongest guarantee. Surprisingly, longer guarantees often have a lower return rate. Your guarantee means you believe in the product and stand behind it. Make is as simple and as powerful as you can.

Your guarantee reassures your buyer. It takes the risk of action away from him or her. If you've offered bonuses, he or she knows they can keep the bonuses but cancel the continuity program or newsletter if they choose. It makes it easier to say YES.

Ideally you want the guarantee both in the text of the email and on the order page. It gains credibility if it looks like a certificate, if it has a signature by it, and if there's a picture of the person who is doing the guaranteeing.

The goal of the guarantee is to remove the risk of action. It lets them know they can change their mind and get their money back if they want to. It makes the decision feel less final. Naturally, when you offer a product of outstanding value, you'll have fewer customers asking for a refund.

6. Call to Action

If you are writing a direct mail renewal, the order device will have your call to action. Throughout the letter, you will invite them to pick up the order form, fill it out and send it back. Then, on the order form, you'll again direct them to take action.

If you are writing an email, you'll want several calls to action throughout the letter. Place an order button near each invitation to make it easy for your reader to act.

Don't discourage the determined buyer by making them read all the way to the end of the letter before they can order. Put an order button early in the letter for those people.

Make your call to action clear and specific. Make it easy for your readers to respond.

You might say, "Click here to renew now." Or if it's an automatic renewal you may need to say, "Do Nothing. Your subscription will easily and automatically renew on its own."

7. Email Series

If your customers are on automatic renewal, you just need one letter to remind them of the upcoming renewal. If, however, your subscribers must choose to renew, you'll need to give them every opportunity to do so.

You cannot count on them taking action the first time they have the opportunity to renew. They may not even open the email. Or perhaps the first email was not convincing enough.

Some readers find it insulting when they receive the same email several times with the same message. If they didn't respond to it the first time, they are not likely to respond to it the second, third, or fifth time. An exception might be if the subject line reads, *"I'm not sure you got this..."* or *"Maybe there was a glitch. Can you check this out again?'* Then it makes sense for them to give it a second reading.

Customers think you are lazy and uncaring when you send the same email over and over. They believe you see them as too stupid to recognize a repeat email—and willing to waste their time. Don't damage the relationship this way.

Set up your email series so it can capture the most variety of customers. Appeal to logic on one. Write to the fear of loss on the next one. Capture future benefits on the third. Set up the urgency to reply with a warning of loss of bonuses on the forth, and so on.

With a series for renewals, it's critical that you have a method of removing the renewing customers from the mailing list. It shows lack of respect and hurts the relationship when the person who has renewed keeps getting renewal notices. You don't need that kind of bad will.

A well-crafted email renewal series can capture and retain customers (and their money) that would otherwise be lost.

CHAPTER 8

Designing the Order Page or Device

Your sale is not complete until the final button is pushed. The fall-off from sales letter to the order page can be considerable. Is it confusing? Different looking... or complicated? Don't scare your buyer off with a complex order page.

Do everything within your power to lead your subscriber or continuity member through the order form to the final click. Here are some ways to make your order page easy, engaging, and effective.

1. Continue the Tone. Don't jar your customer with a change of look, feel, tone or message between the renewal letter and the order page. It should feel seamless. You want them to be in the same frame of mind as they were when reading the letter.

Use similar graphics. Carry on the same tone of voice. Use brief text to remind them once more why they are renewing.

2. Restate the Benefits or Bonuses. You may think you've already said it all in the renewal letter. But the hesitant buyer still has some reservations. Soothe those concerns with a reminder about why this is SUCH a good idea!

3. Keep it Simple. Make it easy to follow. Tell them what they are getting. Capture their information in the simplest way possible. If you have choices—like a 1 year, 3 year, 5 year renewal, lay out the bonuses of each in a clear, easy-to-understand format.

Help them fill it out by giving clear instructions. If they need to enclose a check... remind them.

4. Invite Buy-in. Put the order choices in first person. Move from "you" to "I" in your writing. Instead of saying:

> *You get 12 full color issues of Best Financial Newsletter delivered to your door plus...*

You write:

☐ *Yes! I want 12 full color issues of Best Financial Newsletter delivered...*

When you place it in the first person, the readers feels the excitement and the commitment. They internalize the promises. When they take action by checking the box, they are more likely to stick with it. Your returns go down.

5. Give Several Ways to Order. You want to make it as easy as possible for readers to order in the way that is most comfortable for them.

Decide if tracking is more important than the order. Sometimes readers may prefer to phone in their order. They might rather fax it back or mail it back. Your reader demographics may influence their preferred method. Some are less comfortable giving credit cards online.

Can you give them a variety of online choices? Offer to let them pay with many different credit cards. Accept PayPal, Dwolla, and other less conventional payment methods.

List these payment options along with the information you need from them to complete the order. Make it easy for them to fill out the form... and easy for you to collect the information you need.

If you are writing a direct mail piece, make sure all the information you need from your customer is on one side of the order form. Don't make them write on both sides. They may miss giving you essential information.

Also be sure to give phone and contact information on both the letter and the order form. If they get separated, you still want your reader to be able to make an order.

6. Clear Call to Action. Make it easy for your customers to know what to do. Tell them! Show them. Use graphics— arrows and color— so it's easy to see. Make your order device of a size to fall out of the letter... so they have to pick it up.

On the web page, place an order button close to the top so eager buyers can find it immediately. Some buyers will scroll all the way down... past the guarantee, past all the testimonials, as they decide to finally commit. Make sure there are order buttons along the way— and a final button at the bottom of all the content.

7. Restate the Guarantee. Cautious buyers need the reassurance of a repeat of the guarantee. Spell it out for them again. You can rephrase it into the first person here as well.

I understand I have nothing to lose. I have a 100% MONEYBACK GUARANTEE. If for any reason I am not satisfied I can...

Placing it in first person makes it more real and believable. It instills confidence.

Making it official helps, too. Illustrate it like a certificate. Sign it. Put the signer's picture next to it. Set it off in contrasting color. All these things are proven to increase results.

To the extent you remove the risk from the buyer, you increase the chance of the sale.

8. Testimonials. Social proof helps tip the scale for the fence sitter. In a print order device you have limited space and each must be essential to the message. Online, you have more leeway. You can add testimonial after testimonial down the bottom of the page to reinforce the lingering buyer.

When you have a well-executed order page, your buyers will click on the order button and feel happy doing so. SUCCESS!

Now you move forward once again into retaining your customer.

CHAPTER 9

Writing the Thank You Page

They are sold on your product. At this moment they are happy, satisfied buyers. It's an ideal time to build the relationship. Here are three ways to cement the sale.

1. Genuinely Thank Them. Avoid perfunctory thanks: *Thank you for your order. It will be processed in the next 10 minutes....* Yes, you need to give them instructions for accessing the product. But be genuine. It may sound something like this:

> *Jim- Thanks a lot. I'm really excited to be working with you into the future. I appreciate your trust in me and my process. I promise to work hard for you. I want you to see your wealth increase and your dreams fulfilled.*

Seek to establish that personal connection as you show your appreciation.

2. Show Them the Next Step. What is the next thing they need to do? Is there training they can start? Are there bonuses to unlock and read? Encourage them to take that next step. The sooner they start or continue to engage with your product the more committed they will be.

This is a great time to ask them to read the bonuses. Tell them to download the video and watch it. Give them links, show them benefits. Make it easy for them to do as you ask. Of course you will ask or tell them most respectfully. You will frame it so they understand it's in their best interest.

3. Remind Them of Benefits. Let them know they made the right choice. Confirm their decision as wise and profitable for them. You can do this by reminding them of all the benefits they are going to get because of this decision.

If you do these three steps well, you will cut down on buyer's remorse. You will find your cancelations reduced. Your subscribers will be more likely to take your advice and profit from it. They will become strong advocates for your continuity program or newsletter.

Start the Up-Sell

The thank you page can also be effectively used for upsells. Do not try an upsell before the order is completed. That will typically reduce renewals.

But after the order, the subscriber is in the rosy glow of the purchase. You've spent time helping them make the decision to renew. They are happy with their decision. Now, after the purchase, is the time to offer an upsell.

In your pre-renewal time you considered upsells. What makes the best sense for this particular buyer? Did you offer only a 1 year renewal? Give them a chance to renew for a second year at the same low price. Did they renew for 5 years? Perhaps they are eager to invest in your life-time membership.

Craft the upsell carefully. It might be worded as an exclusive offer reserved only for those who have renewed at that level. It might be offered as an extra benefit to strengthen the value of the renewal.

Be careful not to undercut the recent purchase. Don't ever let buyers feel you are saying, what you just bought really won't do all you want...what you really need is THIS bigger and better program. You risk losing the existing sale and all the lifetime value they can bring you if you do.

Done correctly, however, you will take advantage of the trust and credibility you've built with your subscriber. And you will allow them to strengthen and continue the relationship by letting them learn more from you.

Try a Down-Sell

What if they say no to the upsell? Some savvy marketers give them one more chance with a down-sell. Is there an ancillary product that might appeal?

Perhaps you have an older product that has been off the market for a while. Could you pull it out, brush it off and give it a new life? Might you reposition that product as an aid to help your customer achieve their goals easier and faster?

Look for something you could offer at a low price point. Try one more time to present another offer of a product that would benefit them.

The thank you page is critical real estate on your website. It should do WAY more than confirm the sale and give directions. Its purpose is to:

Cement and build upon the relationship
- Reduce buyer's remorse
- Start the engagement process

- Offer an opportunity to become even more involved with you through upsells

Review every thank you page you use to insure you are getting the very most from it. Use the checklist to see that you are capturing every benefit.

When you fully employ the thank you page you will see customer satisfaction increase, returns reduce, and profits rise. Take advantage of this opportunity.

CHAPTER 10

When They Say No: Creating the Win-Back Series

N ot every subscriber is going to renew. What then? Studies show that someone who has purchased from you is much more likely to purchase from you again. More so than a new customer.

Chances are you have thousands of former customers who once subscribed... but no longer do. Those lists still have value. Will they all come back? Of course not. But there is gold among the dross. Don't leave that money buried in old lists.

Pull out the gold— the customers who still need and want your program— with a win-back series.

Plan on a longer series of email than you might typically offer. If it's been more than a few months since they were customers, you'll need to re-warm the list. They need to get reacquainted with you and what you offer. They must once again discover why they liked you, trusted you, and wanted to do business with you.

Here are eight ways to connect with your customers and bring them back.

---

1. Why Did They Leave?

Here, especially, it is so helpful to understand the mind of your prospective renewers. What made them drop out? No time? No money? No interest? Problem solved? It's possible they've moved to another source and the problem HAS been solved. In that case, you are out of luck.

But more likely, the concern that brought them to your newsletter is still there. As you rekindle that pain and worry, you can remind them of how important it is to find a workable solution. And you must show them why your newsletter or continuity program is in their best interest.

One first step can be a survey. It can help you determine why your subscribers didn't renew. It gives you insight into their thoughts and decision process. It also offers people in your old list a chance to "raise their hand" and let you know they are still interested.

Those who respond to the survey are more likely to engage with you again. These are your most likely prospects. A request to help with your survey must be respectful, appreciative, and clear. They need to know what to expect and what the benefit to them will be. It might look like this.

> *Jim, in the past you subscribed to Best Financial Newsletter. I respect your intellect and rational. Could I possibly impose on you to take 3 minutes and tell me your thoughts on Best Financial Newsletter and why you are no longer with us?*
>
> *I want to ask just two simple questions:*

1. What did you hope to gain when you subscribed to Best Financial Newsletter?

2. And what led you to stop subscribing?

You can hit reply to answer on this email, or click here to go to a survey site.

As a thank you for your time, include your address and we'll happily send you [nice product] typically reserved for our platinum members only.

Surveys need to be very clear that you are not going to try to sell them something. Readers must be confident they will not be lured in under the pretense that you want their advice only to be sold to.

---

2. Show Them What They Are Missing

Noted business consultant and strategic marketer, Jay Abraham, says to start with the assumption that the people you are writing to will become a customer again. Start giving them valuable information for free. Investment newsletter customers typically receive teaser emails. They say in effect:

We have this marvelous, exciting information that will be a disaster for you if you don't have it. But we're not going to give it to you unless you subscribe.

As subscribers get more sophisticated, they also get more jaded and resentful. Imagine the relationship tool of actually giving them the valuable information. Not all of it, of course. But real, actionable information.

You might say:

This week we are giving you a taste of Best Financial Newsletter. For this week only we are letting you in on current insider tips, actionable stock picks, and our rational behind recommending them. Feel free to use every pick and profit from it.

We hope you will find our stocks so profitable and so exciting you want to rejoin the Best Financial Newsletter family. At the end of the week, we'll have a special offer for you. But even if you don't choose to keep up with us, we want you to have this valuable information for free.

This letter is very transparent and respectful. It lets readers know they are getting exactly the same information as the regular newsletter subscriber with no strings attached. You're up front that you'll invite them to join your newsletter at the end. It gives them confidence they'll have an opportunity to continue if they wish. But you show them the material is entirely free and separate from any commitment they may make.

It may be that readers are already getting a daily free newsletter from you. You might consider a reverse offer. You might send an alert letting them know you are reviewing subscribers to the free letter and ask them if they want to continue. When you require them to take action, you uncover clients willing to do more business with you.

Or try sending a survey about the value of the free content. Again, those who respond are "raising their hand." They may be interested in ascending to a paid subscription.

You could then follow up with a targeted letter explaining the difference between the free and the paid subscription. Because if what you leaned in the survey, you have the insight to motivate them with reasons they should move up to the paid subscription NOW.

3. Invite Them Back with Proof and Credibility

As you re-warm your old customers, you'll need to remind them just how good you are. Your emails or letters will include proof of the benefits you've given to customers just like them. You'll want to explain again how smart and powerful your expert is.

In a field crowded with over 2000 newsletters, you'll need to differentiate yourself. Of course newsletters divide out into conservative and aggressive investors, market sectors, options and such. Even so, there are probably a dozen or more newsletters doing exactly what you do.

What is your unique selling proposition? Your expert. His guidance and his take on the market may be duplicated. But his personality, his relationship with the customer cannot be. Part of your credibility process is to build that sense of trust between reader and guru.

Does the expert fulfill his or her promises? Does the track record support the claims? Statistics, graphs, charts, and specific information all help build that trust and credibility.

4. Use Emotions

Many buyers like to imagine they make decisions based on facts. However, the truth is purchasing or investing is often an emotional decision. Ultimately, people don't want a product, they want a solution to their pain—their problem.

When the stock market tumbles even "logical and rational" investors feel the gut wrench, worry and fear that erupts into irrational behavior. Financial newsletter readers look to an expert to shield them from that fear and panic. They want promises that if they follow that expert they can find peace, financial security, a comfortable retirement, and dreams fulfilled.

People who buy other continuity products want that same safety and promise that if they follow the steps, they'll achieve their goals.

Successful win-back series draw on those emotions. They may be given voice in testimonials and stories. The expert's rags-to-riches story may resonate with them and give credibility. The stories of other subscribers who have followed the advice and reaped great benefits also reassure readers they can succeed, too. When the testimonies share the reader's pain points and the joy and security of success they invite imitation.

Not every reader has the same goal or the same emotional pull. Carefully craft your win-back series to draw upon different emotions in different emails. The email one reader might skim and delete—because it's too logical or emotional— might be just the trigger that causes another reader to believe and subscribe.

Use a Marketing Sales Funnel approach. Your win-back series must cover a lot of ground. You want to take your readers through these steps:

- Reacquaint them with you
- Start building trust, credibility, and relationships
- Make an irresistible offer
- Lead them to want to buy
- Create urgency

5. Make an Irresistible Offer

Marketing experts say your sales depend on the offer (40%), the list (40%) and the strength of the sales letter (20%). Since your win-back list is not as strong as your active member list, better results will come as you craft a potent offer.

Evaluate the lifetime value of your customers to see how much of a discount you can give them on the front end product. Review their needs to find a promotion that will resonate with them.

Chances are you've used the standard *Throw-a-Zillion-Bonuses-at-Them* promo and found some success with that approach. It's common to gift a free trial of a companion newsletter as well. What other offers might you try that are less common?

- A physical product that relates to your offer— calculator, stock option record book, clock or wallet
- A downloadable tool that will make your product easier to use— like a stock evaluator and instructional videos on how to use it
- A video of an inside look into the research of the expert
- Back door access to past advice— perhaps stock picks and how they performed
- Invitation to an investment seminar or webinar
- Joining a club or insider community

Remember the offer should fill a need they believe they have. They need to see the connection between the offer and the solution to the problem they are facing. The more you understand their worry, fears and pain, the better you can create an offer that will be truly irresistible. It will so mesh with their core needs they will be anxious to get started.

6. Create Urgency

We are a world of procrastinators. And, indeed, we look for excuses to not part with our money. We may even be slow to do things we KNOW are good for us.

To help overcome that inertia, you need to provide incentive for them to act. To act NOW! This is easy to do if you only open up your continuity program or subscription for a few weeks each year. This is how Jeff Walker of Product Launch Formula creates urgency and scarcity.

But how do you handle renewals or win-back series that can occur at any time of the year? With auto-responder email series, each time a reader steps into the system, it's a new "sale" to him or her. Here are six ways to create scarcity and urgency to buy right away.

Limit Time. The sale price is only available for a specific amount of time to this subscriber. It's helpful if you can justify the time period. Jaded readers think if it can be sold for $89 this week, why can't it be sold for $89 next week? Give them a reason.

New! If a product, survey, stock pick etc. has JUST come out. There is an urgency to get it before it gets old, stale, or outdated.

Limit Number. If you only have 1000 copies of the book, there's an urgency to get them before they are sold out.

Take Away Bonuses. You can create an offer for a product that will continue at that price, but after a certain time, they can no longer get the bonuses for free. Again, to avoid having your reader feel jerked around, you'll need to come up with a valid reason for the bonuses to disappear.

Countdown Timer. This adds a sense of urgency when used with limited time or limited number offers. There is something hypnotic and panic inducing about watching the timer run down. You want to act now!

Take Away the Product. This works well in an exclusive offer. You may invite people to join your continuity program or newsletter, but you're limiting the time for people to join. After that time, the investment opportunity or program will be closed and will not accept new members.

You can use a combination of these to build up the urgency and value such that your prospective clients can't wait to join your program or subscription.

---

7. Cross-sell

Some people on your list are simply not interested in the offer you are making to them. For whatever reason, after you've warmed them, explained credibility, built trust, and made them an irresistible offer... and they've turned you down.

If this product is not of interest to them, what else can you offer them? Your first tendency is to offer them another one of your own newsletters. Some will take advantage of those offers. What else can you offer that they might feel solves their primary concern?

If you sell stock market picks, you know they are interested in finance and wealth growth but they are not biting on growth stocks, dividend stocks, mining and gold stocks, options, or anything else you've offered. Think of complementary services to your business.

Can you partner with a company that deals with a different kind of finance, investment or savings to offer them another way to accomplish their dreams and goals? For example, in the financial sector could you offer information or access to:

- Money saving tips, travel discounts, etc.
- Physical gold, silver or precious metals
- Real estate investments
- Mortgages and liens

- Business investments
- Annuities and life insurance
- Self-directed IRA's
- Budgeting or money managing growth strategies
- Financial education for their children

Offers along these lines may salvage a lost customer and bring them back into your sphere of influence. When you bring solutions your customers want— even if it is outside your company— you build trust and strengthen your relationship. And with joint ventures or affiliate programs you also share in the profits of the purchase.

---

8. Down-sells

Pull out the list you created in Chapter 6 on the down-sell. If readers have rejected your other offers, try a very small price-point offer. Maybe you offer one specific item for $5 or $7 dollars that has a much greater true value.

This may draw your reader back into becoming a customer. And again, once they are an active customer... they are more likely to buy from you again.

Win-back series capture money that's been left on the table from your old outdated lists of former customers. They can be a lucrative infusion of cash for you. Indeed, if you've ignored this list, it is essentially free cash for you!

CHAPTER 11

Building the Support System

R etaining customers depends in large measure on your customer support system. You can do an effective job of building trust and strengthening relationship in your newsletters and your retention programs. But if your customer service lacks the right tone and follow-through, it can quickly destroy any benefits to you.

- Phone rings... and rings... and rings and no one answers?
- Recording after recording and hard to get a live person?
- Unhelpful support staff?
- They can't answer your customer's questions?

All these lead to unhappy former customers and create a disconnect between the warm relationship you are trying to build and the reality of the business they see, hear, and feel.

Customer service people are the front-line of the company. They deserve quality pay, excellent training and positive support. A strong customer service department can reduce cancelations and increase your profits. They are also in a position to give you feedback on the pulse of the clients.

How can you help your customer service do more for retentions?

1. Avoid "No Questions Asked" Guarantees. You want your customer service to be able to ask questions of customers who call to cancel. No one wants to be bullied back into keeping the service, but it is possible to respectfully comply with the customer's request to cancel and still engage them in a dialogue about the product.

The first step is to agree to... and process the cancelation request. Make sure the customer knows that you are willing and in the process of canceling their subscription. When they know they will not need to fight to have the subscription canceled, they are more disposed to answer other questions.

The dialogue might go something like this:

> *Of course, Mr. Smart, I'm happy to cancel your subscription to Best Financial Newsletter. I am processing the order as we speak.*
>
> *Mr. Smart, here at Best Financial Publications, we strive to give the most current and valuable content possible. What could we have done to make Best Financial Newsletter more valuable to you?*

Essentially you are taking an exit survey. Your goal is to gather information that will help you keep future customers. You might ask questions like:

- What motivated you to try the newsletter?
- What did you like about our service or product?
- Which parts of the newsletter, product, or continuity program did you find most useful?
- What led you to discontinue the subscription?
- Is there anything we could do at this point to bring you back as a subscriber?

Of course you are aware that some may not want to share and some will not be forthcoming with the truth. Make sure your tone of voice is inviting and accepting of their honest answers. Phrase the questions so customers feel comfortable declining to answer if they prefer. If you give them an out, the answers you receive are more likely to be accurate.

2. Scripts. Sometimes it's hard to come up with the correct words— words that will be honoring, respectful, supportive and clear. When support staff has to think on their feet it's more likely that inappropriate comments or phrases may come out of their mouths and damage the company reputation.

Help your call center customer support staff succeed by giving them scripts to use. They need not be locked onto the script and use it word-for-word. You don't want them to sound stilted or robotic. But they can be very handy to clarify a general reply or frame a response in the most positive way.

Scripts can be a lifesaver when the correct words do not flow easily. And they can be essential in saving a sale or creating a new sale.

3. Support the Side-Sell. Ryan Deiss, owner of Digital Marketer, strives hard to build a loyal tribe of fans who buy his products. He offers a side-sell to those who want to return a product. This four step process is guaranteed to have your customers loving you and increases the likelihood they will continue as lifelong buyers.

Step one. His customer support staff asks the person if they are still struggling with the problem that led them to buy the product. Chances are, they still have the problem.

Step two. The staff then, while reaffirming their willingness to cancel the order and refund the money, offers an option to switch— at no charge— to another product that might better help the customer achieve his or her goal.

Step three. They discuss the other products in their line or with their affiliates to find the best one for the current customer and their situation.

Step four. They offer to let the customer try the new program for 30 days to test it out. Then the customer can decide to cancel the product and receive a refund, or they can change over to the new product and the company keeps their money.

Imagine the good public relations this engenders. The client finds a support staff that genuinely wants to help them solve the problem they are facing. They don't feel like someone is just trying to sell them something.

When they feel like their worries, concerns and problems are properly listened to and addressed the customer feels valued. When customer service lets the client try the product— cost free— for a month before making up his or her mind, the customer feels the company has gone above and beyond what was expected.

Businesses gain the distinct advantage of saving some sales. But even if customers cancel, they continue to feel good about you and your company. You've created superior trust and long-lasting memories of a good relationship. Friends tell other people when they've been treated exceptionally well.

4. Increase Testimonials. Train your support staff to invite testimonials and record them. Help them learn how to get "the whole story" of the success— from problem through solution. Encourage them to ask questions that highlight the benefits that came to the client because of the product.

Teach them to uncover the emotions beneath the success— peace, security, confidence, empowerment. Can they create a visual picture or specific details that reveal the emotions through tangible results? People might say things like:

- We love the fact that we can visit grandkids whenever we want
- We have the freedom to travel to Europe each year
- Our house is paid off and we feel such a sense of security
- I don't stay up at night worrying if we'll run out of money before we run out of living

When these emotions can be woven into the testimonial they resonate with readers and increase the power of the testimonial.

If you can get your call staff to save and categorize these testimonials every time they get them, the staff will be a huge support to the retention side of the business.

4. Honor Your Support Staff. Use your customer support staff to strengthen your products. Include them in your product development and in building retention. Ask for their insights, their gut feelings, and their assessment of why customers are dropping out and what can be done to fix it.

Customer support staff and call staff are the ears of the company. Value them and use them.

CHAPTER 12

Growing Income with Retention, Renewals, Win-backs & Up-Sells

F ar too many companies treat retention like a sadly neglected step-child. Front end sales get the money, the dazzle, and the preferential treatment. But that is a short-sighted view. It permits money to drain away instead of reclaiming and holding onto it. When companies spend a little more time and money on retention— when they create a system to follow— they can reduce attrition and plug the hole in their leaky bucket.

Attrition is a part of every business. But the degree of loss can be reduced by careful attention to retention and renewal. When you devote time and energy to retention, you increase income without as much time and money spent filling the funnel of new customers.

You have more paying customers for a longer time. They move up to higher cost products. They send friends and family to buy from you.

Start the renewal process at the time of the sale. Warmly welcome them to your business "family." Remind them of the great deal they got and let them know how smart they were to choose your product and expert.

Then find ways to get them immediately involved with the product. Increase their skills and learning. Lead them through the process of understanding your product and how to take advantage of it. Invite questions and feedback. Treat them with honor.

Keeping Customers is More Profitable than Getting New Ones

A great general said that it's easier to keep a city then to try and recapture it. The same holds true for your clients. Be prepared to spend as much time and money on retention as you did on getting the customer in the first place. If you lose them... you'll HAVE to spend that much money getting a new customer to replace them.

Don't let them slip away because of your inactivity. Watch out for customers that are at risk. Intervene early to recapture their interest and involvement and learn what is causing their detachment. Then find a work-around.

Put your personality and unique strengths on display as part of your unique selling proposition. Be quirky. Send surprise gifts. Shower customers with valuable content. Then take them smoothly through the renewal process so they remain contented customers— or better yet, eager customers who want to buy everything you offer them.

Build a customer support system that works hand-in-glove with the retention process. Use the strengths of your customer service to learn more about your customers and to help them find the best product for their needs.

Finally, go and rescue those who have jumped ship. Seek out the gold in the old lists of former customers. Create a plan to reignite their interest in you and your products. As you work toward a solution to their worries and concerns, they come to appreciate and value you.

Even if you need to turn them over to a complementary or joint venture service, they will feel respected and honored. That pays unexpected dividends.

Retention is a way of thinking. It's a way of appreciating and valuing customers— not just for the cash they bring in, but for who they are. When you care about their goals, needs, and desires, you will elevate your entire business.

It is also a system. As you strengthen each part of the system you make a difference in the bottom line. Work to put every one of the retention and renewal devices in place, you'll create a well-oiled, duplicating machine. You can be confident you are not leaving any money on the table. It's all going into your pocket.

That's a feeling that never gets old.

Author Bio: Sandy Fox

"Value and relationships are the heart of every long-term business transaction. Customers and clients remain loyal when they receive valuable content and are treated with respect and care. It works for retentions and renewals, and it works for my long-term clients as well.'—Sandy Fox*

Sandy Fox specializes in writing retention, renewal, win-back and upsells for financial newsletters and other continuity programs. She helps clients grow their business through retention and increasing customer lifetime value.

She draws on a wide range of training from master copywriters, marketers, and business leaders— Bob Bly, Clayton Makepeace, Dan Kennedy, Ryan Deiss, Chris Marlow, Jeff Walker, AWAI and others. Using techniques found in a broad range of businesses and marketing allow her to "cross-pollinate." This brings new ideas and practices into your retentions and renewals that give you an edge over the competition.

Her investing experience spans more than 30 years and includes stocks, bonds, mutual funds, ETF's, options, metals, and alternative investments in real estate, mortgages and private lending.

Sandy Fox has been writing persuasively since 1993 mastering storytelling and reader connection through stories and articles for print magazines.

Working with editors means she understands collaboration, editorial direction, creating the right voice and tone—and meeting deadlines!

Interested in cashing in on the returns from retention, renewals, win-backs and up-sells? Contact Sandy Fox.

Sandy@InvestmentCopy.com

www.InvestmentCopy.com

870 491-5505 (office) 870-565-7700 (cell)

Printed in Great Britain
by Amazon